# COWBOYS

## CHARLES SULLIVAN

An ADVENTURES IN ART Book

# Once Upon a Horse

Once upon his faithful horse
a cowboy rode the range,
and hoped the country that he loved
would never, never change.

Now time has passed,
but good things last—
the West is still the West—
so come with me
and you will see
the cowboy's life is best!

Frederic Remington (1861–1909).
Painter, sculptor, author who moved to
the West and captured the color and
activity of Western life better than any
other artist of his time.

*The Cowboy* by
Frederic Remington,
1902

# The Cowboy's Life

The cowboy's life
is the life for me
as soon as I can ride!
I'll get my jeans
and boots and spurs
and wear them all with pride!

Barbara Van Cleve (Born 1935).
Montana rancher who "lives
her photographs" to show us
what the West and its people
are really like today.

*Chinks, Oxbow and Jinglebobs*
(cowboy names for leather
overalls, a wooden stirrup, and
spurs). Photograph by Barbara
Van Cleve, 1984

*Cliffs of the Upper Colorado River, Wyoming Territory* by Thomas Moran, 1882

# I Love
# the West

I love the West
    'cause it's so big
that nothing there
        looks small;
I love the way
        the mountains rise
so beautiful and tall;
I love the plains
        and deserts, too,
and every kind of stream,
and when I fall asleep
        at night
the West is what I dream!

Thomas Moran (1837–1926).
Eastern artist who fell in love
with the West, especially its
panoramic mountains and
canyons, which he portrayed
in large, idealized landscapes.

# Racing for a Watermelon

Cowboys are happy
chasing cows,
or racing for a prize—
    maybe a new *sombrero,*
    or an old one, if it's nice,
or a Mexican watermelon
of more than average size.

Theodore Gentilz (1819–1906).
Artist, teacher who came to the
United States from France in
1844, liked what he saw, and
settled in San Antonio, Texas.

*The Watermelon Race* by Theodore Gentilz, 1890

*Storytelling on the Matador Ranch, Texas.* Photograph by Erwin Evans Smith, 1910

# Campfire at Night

When the sun has set
and their work is done,
cowboys gather one by one.

As the campfire burns
they take turns
with a joke or a song or a
    story
of the West in all its glory.

Erwin Evans Smith (1886–1947).
Photographer who recorded many
authentic scenes of ranch life while
working as a cowboy in Texas, New
Mexico, and Arizona.

*Old Bull* by Alexander Calder, 1930

# Some Cows Are Really Bulls

A cow is a she,
a bull is a he,
and I'm glad that neither
is now chasing me!

Alexander Calder (1898–1976).
Sculptor, painter who used a wide
variety of materials to produce
amusing images of animals and
people before turning to larger, more
abstract "mobiles" and other works.

*The Strenuous Life* by Charles M. Russell, 1901

# Driving
# the Cattle

Cows and bulls
are all called *"cattle,"*
and rounding them up
is quite a battle!

Moving them on
is called a *"drive"*—
you've never seen anything
so alive!

Charles M. Russell (1864–1926).
Cowboy artist who remained a
cowboy in spite of his artistic
success, as we can see in the
illustrated letters he wrote to his
friends (see page 25).

# The End of the Cattle Drive

Sometimes it's easy
and sometimes it's hard,
sometimes you'd rather
stay home in your yard.

Sometimes it's dusty
and sometimes there's
    rain,
sometimes the cattle
won't climb on the train.

But sooner or later
the cattle drive ends
and the cowboys ride
    back
to the ranch with their
    friends.

Thomas Hart Benton (1889–1975). Painter whose belief in the importance of ordinary people and everyday events is reflected in his lively scenes of regional life in America.

*Cattle Loading, West Texas* by Thomas Hart Benton, 1930

# Who's Boss—
# The Cowboy
# or the Hoss?

*"Busting a bronco"*
means teaching a wild horse
new habits,
so it won't throw riders off,
or bite their knees,
or gallop through the cactus
chasing rabbits!

*The Bronco Buster* by
Frederic Remington, 1895

# Some Cowboys Are Really Cowgirls

I heard about a cowgirl
out in Utah, nicknamed "Tad,"
who rode a horse from Canada
'cause he was big and bad.
He knew a hundred wicked tricks,
and he would try them all,
but Tad stayed in the saddle—
he couldn't make her fall!

*Tad Lucas on "Juarez,"*
*Salt Lake City, Utah.*
Photograph, 1924

# **Roping a Calf Isn't Easy**

Roping a calf isn't really
as simple as it looks—
that smart little critter could
    teach you
more than your cowboy books!

Keith Williams (Born 1949). Kentucky
newspaper photographer whose pictures
are included in the widely acclaimed
*Songs of My People* exhibition and book.

*World Champion Calf-Roper Fred
Whitfield, Cleburne, Texas.*
Photograph by Keith Williams, 1990

# Riding the Stage Coach

Back in the days
before cars or trains,
people traveled other ways
across the Western plains.

They had all kinds of wagons,
but nothing could approach
the excitement of riding
in an old stage coach!

*The Old Stage Coach of the Plains*
by Frederic Remington, 1901

# Catching the Outlaws

The best old Western movies
are the ones that star John Wayne—
just when you think he's down and out,
he gets back up again!
He often plays the "good guy"
who chases someone bad,
but when he finally catches them
he looks a little sad.

Harry Jackson (Born 1924).
Wyoming sculptor, one of the
first contemporary artists to
use paint on bronze; he was
born in Chicago but left
home at age fourteen to
become a cowboy.

*The Marshal* by
Harry Jackson, 1970

*Cowboys at Home Ranch* by Thomas Eakins, 1888

# Cowboy Song

Swinging in the saddle
all day long,
you can hear me singing
a cowboy song—
the same old words
and the same old tune,
about the cattle herds
and the rising moon,
and the night that's falling
soon—too soon.

Thomas Eakins (1844–1916).
Eastern artist, known for
masterful portraits and sporting
scenes, who painted several
Western pictures after a brief
visit in the 1880s.

# Could I Be a Cowboy?

I'd like to be a cowboy
riding fast,
not in the movies,
not in the past,
but right here, right *now*—
if I could only find a cow!

*Against the Sunset* by
Frederic Remington, 1906

43

Title page illustration: Smith, Erwin Evans, *Cattle Drive on the JA Ranch, Texas,* 1907. Photograph.

First published in the United States of America in 1993 by
Rizzoli International Publications, Inc.
300 Park Avenue South, New York, N.Y. 10010

Library of Congress Cataloging-in-Publication Data

Sullivan, Charles, 1933–
    Cowboys / Charles Sullivan.
       p.   cm.   — (An Adventures in Art book)
    Summary: The author's original poems are illustrated
with photographs and with famous paintings by Frederic
Remington, Charles Russell, and others.
    ISBN 0-8478-1680-X
    1. Cowboys—Juvenile poetry.   2. Cowboys in art—
Juvenile literature.   3. Children's poetry, American.
[1. Cowboys—Poetry.   2. Cowboys in art.   3. American
poetry.]   I. Title.   II. Series.
PS3569.U345C68   1993
811'.54—dc20                      92–42980
                                         CIP
                                         AC

Design by Gilda Hannah

Printed in Singapore